SRA Reading Mastery
Signature Edition

Literature Anthology

Siegfried Engelmann
Susan Hanner

McGraw Hill SRA

Columbus, OH

Acknowledgements

Grateful acknowledgement is given to the following publishers and copyright owners for permissions granted to reprint selections from their publications. All possible care has been taken to trace ownership and secure permission for each selection included. In case of any errors or omissions, the Publisher will be pleased to make suitable acknowledgements in future editions.

Candlewick Press
A CARIBBEAN DOZEN
"The Runner" © 1994 Faustin Charles
Compilation © 1994 John Agard & Grace Nichols.
Reproduced by permission of Candlewick Press Inc., Cambridge, MA.

Harcourt
"A Lucky Thing" from A LUCKY THING, copyright © 1999, 1997 by Alice Schertle, used with permission of Harcourt, Inc.

HarperCollins
AMELIA BEDELIA by Peggy Parish. TEXT COPYRIGHT © 1963 by MARGARET PARISH PICTURES COPYRIGHT ©1963 by FRITZ SIEBERT Used by permission of HarperCollins Publishers.

THE SOUP STONE by Maria Leach COPYRIGHT © 1954 BY FUNK & WAGNALLS CO. Used by permission of HarperCollins Publishers.

"The Pancake Collector" From THE QUEEN OF EENE TEXT COPYRIGHT © 1978 by JACK PRELUTSKY
Used by permission of HarperCollins Publishers.

Mike Makley
The New Kid, by Mike Makley © 1975.

"Dreams" copyright © 1994 by The Estate of Langston Hughes, from THE COLLECTED POEMS OF LANGSTON HUGHES by Langston Hughes. Used by permission of Alfred A. Knopf, a division of Random House, Inc.

Simon & Schuster
"Spaghetti" Reprinted with the permission of Atheneum Books for Young Readers, an imprint of Simon & Schuster Children's Publishing Division from EVERY LIVING THING by Cynthia Rylant. Copyright © 1985 Cynthia Rylant.

"Boar Out There" Reprinted with the permission of Atheneum Books for Young Readers, an imprint of Simon & Schuster Children's Publishing Division from EVERY LIVING THING by Cynthia Rylant. Copyright © 1985 Cynthia Rylant.

Thomson Learning Australia
CHARLIE BEST by Ruth Corrin and JULIE RESCUES BIG MACK by Roger Hall used by permission of Thomson Learning Australia.

Won-Ldy Paye
WHY LEOPARD HAS BLACK SPOTS by Won-Ldy Paye. Copyright © 1991 by Won-Ldy Paye. Used by permission of the author.

NOT JUST ANY RING by Danita Ross Haller copyright © 1982 by Danita Ross Haller and Alfred A Knopf, Inc. Pictures by Deborah Kogan Ray. Published by arrangement with Alfred A Knopf Books for Young Readers, an imprint of Random House Children's Books, a division of Random House, Inc., New York, New York. All rights reserved.

SRAonline.com

Printed in the United States of America.

Send all inquiries to this address:
SRA/McGraw-Hill
4400 Easton Commons
Columbus, OH 43219

ISBN: 978-0-07-612583-8
MHID: 0-07-612583-1

4 5 6 7 8 9 10 11 QPD 13 12 11 10 09 08

TABLE OF CONTENTS

TABLE OF CONTENTS
continued

The Velveteen Rabbit

Retold by Harriet Winfield • Illustrated by José Miralles

Timmy was a little boy who had lots of toys, and he liked to play with all of them. But his favorite toy was the velveteen rabbit that he received on his fourth birthday.

Oh, how he loved that soft
cuddly rabbit. At night, he could
not go to sleep unless he snuggled
up with the rabbit close to his body.
When he played out in the yard, he
always had that rabbit with him. He
even talked to his velveteen rabbit.

After a while, the rabbit started to show
signs of wear. It became tattered and torn.
One of its ears no longer stood up. And its
color had changed from a pretty pink color to
gray. But Timmy loved it even more than when
he had first held it.

Timmy's mother tried to interest Timmy in other toys. She wanted to get rid of the velveteen rabbit because she thought it was dirty and ugly. She said, "Why don't you give me the rabbit, and I'll get you a fine new animal to play with."

"No," Timmy said. "This rabbit is not like the others. This rabbit is real."

"Real?" his mother said. "He's just a toy."

"No," Timmy insisted. "He's real."

The next day, Timmy was playing with the tattered rabbit in the yard when it started to rain. Timmy went inside, but he forgot to take the rabbit with him. When it was time for Timmy to go to bed, he remembered where the rabbit was. He snuck outside in the rain and cold and searched for the rabbit until he found it. Then he hugged his rabbit and said, "You are cold and wet, but I will make you feel better." He took the rabbit inside, dried it, and took it to bed with him. He snuggled up and went to sleep.

A few days later, Timmy became very sick. He had a high fever and strange dreams. In one of his dreams a lovely princess appeared. She said, "The love your rabbit has for you will make you well. And your love for the rabbit will make him real."

Timmy got well, and he remembered what the princess had said. But as the months passed, the poor rabbit became even shabbier than it had been. Part of its stuffing was coming out, and it had a large rip on its back.

One day, Timmy's mother said, "Timmy, you are a big boy now. It's time for you to get rid of that rabbit. It's falling apart."

Timmy said, "But a princess told me that this rabbit will become a real rabbit."

His mother said, "Then why don't you take him out into the woods and leave him there, where he can live with the other rabbits."

Sadly, Timmy agreed. With tears in his eyes, he took his tattered velveteen rabbit to the woods. He put it down in soft leaves, next to a large tree. He patted it and said, "I . . . I have to leave you here . . . but you will be fine. . . . You will be a real rabbit."

He started to walk away, but after he took a few steps he turned around to look at his rabbit for the last time. To his surprise, the tattered rabbit was gone. And sitting in its place was a bunny—a real rabbit.

The bunny hopped over to Timmy and seemed to smile. "Oh," Timmy cried. "You are real." Then the bunny hopped over to where two other bunnies were playing. They welcomed their new friend, and the three of them hopped off.

Timmy often went back into the woods to
watch his bunny play with the other rabbits.
Although it had changed, Timmy knew that his
velveteen rabbit would always love him as much
as he loved it.

Dreams

by Langston Hughes
Illustrated by Anni Matsick

Hold fast to dreams
For if dreams die
Life is a broken-winged bird
That cannot fly.

Hold fast to dreams
For when dreams go
Life is a barren field
Frozen with snow.

The Runner

by Faustin Charles

Illustrated by Kate Flanagan

Run, run, runner man,
As fast as you can,
Faster than the speed of light,
Smoother than a bird in flight.
Run, run, runner man,
No one can catch the runner man,
Swifter than an arrow,
Outrunning his own shadow.
Run, run, runner man,
Faster than tomorrow.
Run, run, runner man,
Quicker than a rocket!
Into deep space spinning a comet!
Run, run, runner man,
Lighting the heavens of the night,
Run, run, runner man,
Out of sight,
Run, run, runner man, run!

The Emperor's New Clothes

Retold by Harvey Cleaver

Illustrated by Jenny Williams

Once there lived a very rich and powerful emperor. The emperor was a kind and good-hearted ruler, but he had a strange interest. He loved clothes, and he had more clothes than anyone in the land. He had so many clothes that they filled most of the closets and rooms in his palace. The emperor had three tailors who spent all their time making new clothes for him.

The emperor spent his time differently. He loved to look at himself in his fine clothing. The halls of the palace were lined with mirrors, and every room had several large mirrors so the emperor could see himself wherever he went in the palace.

One day a clever thief came to the palace. The
thief was dressed like a tailor. He told the guards that
he had the finest fabric the emperor had ever seen.

A guard led the thief to the emperor. The thief quickly told the emperor, "You must not let your other tailors know about the fabric I have to show you. If they know, they will become very jealous and will make up lies to try to change the way you think about the suit I can make for you."

The emperor said, "The other tailors will not know about the fabric or the suit."

The thief said, "The fabric I will show you is not only wonderful—it is magic. Only the wisest people in the land can see this fabric. Fools will not see it. To them, the fabric will look invisible."

The thief opened his bag and pretended to hold up some fabric. "There," the thief said. "Isn't that magnificent?"

Of course, the emperor could see nothing. But he did not admit that he saw nothing, because he did not want to look like a fool. So he pretended to see a wonderful fabric. "Oh, oh, isn't that exciting," he said. "Yes, it is wonderful."

The thief pretended to make a fine suit of clothes with pants, a jacket, and a robe. Then the thief pretended to hand the clothes to the emperor, and the emperor pretended to put them on. The emperor paid the thief 20 gold coins for the new suit. This was more than he had ever paid for a suit, but the thief reminded him that nobody had ever seen such a suit before.

The queen was shocked when she saw the emperor standing naked in front of the mirror. He said, "My queen, I know that you can see my wonderful new clothes because you are no fool. Fools cannot see this magic fabric, but I'm sure that you can."

"Oh, indeed I can," she said. "It's very unusual, isn't it?"

The emperor was afraid to take off
his magic suit that night because he was
afraid that he would not be able to see it
or even feel it again.

The next day, the emperor ordered a great
parade so he could show everybody in the land
his wonderful new clothes.

People came from all over. Most of them had already heard that fools were not able to see the magic fabric, so when they saw the naked emperor passing by in his splendid carriage, they made flattering comments. "My, my, what a handsome suit," they said. "It's like nothing I've ever seen before." But the people who lined the streets did not cheer the way they would cheer if they saw something wonderful. After they pretended to see something wonderful, they quickly became quiet, staring at the emperor with puzzled eyes.

If the crowd had not been so quiet, people probably would not have heard what the little child said. As the emperor neared the busiest street on the parade route, a little child looked up at the emperor and asked, "Mother, why doesn't the emperor have any clothes on?"

The people in the crowd heard the child. So did the emperor. In an instant, he knew the child was right. The emperor realized that he was naked. In the same instant, all the people in the crowd realized that they had been fools for not saying what they actually saw. At first only a few of them laughed, but the laughter swelled, and soon the sound of people laughing was deafening. The emperor nearly died of embarrassment. He darted from the carriage and ran all the way back to his palace, but he could still hear the laughter.

For three weeks after that day, he did not leave the palace or see anyone. When he finally came out of hiding, he had changed. He didn't care as much about clothes, and he was a wiser ruler. From that bitter parade, he had learned a valuable lesson: pretending does not change the way things really are.

Why Leopard Has Black Spots

Told by Won-Ldy Paye

Edited by Margaret H. Lippert, Illustrated by Ted Eink

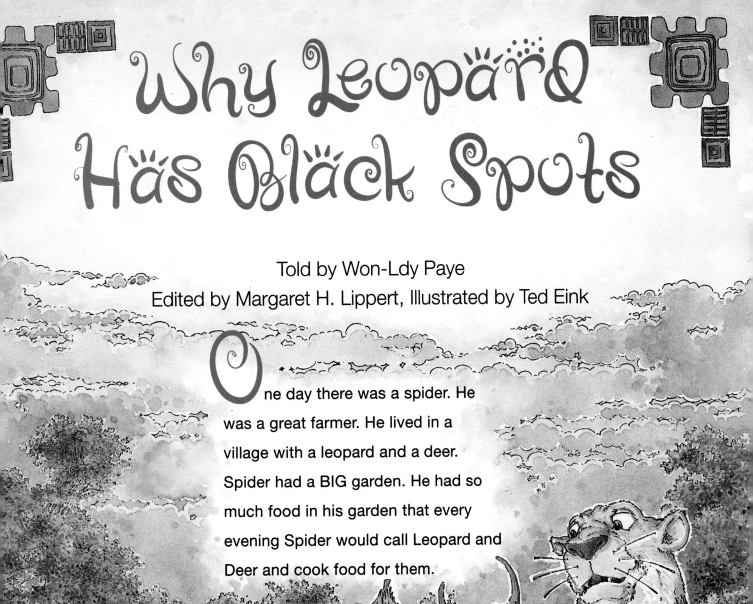

One day there was a spider. He was a great farmer. He lived in a village with a leopard and a deer. Spider had a BIG garden. He had so much food in his garden that every evening Spider would call Leopard and Deer and cook food for them.

But one day Spider went to his garden and noticed something was different. "Something is missing," he thought. Day after day things seemed to be missing.

At first he didn't care, because his garden was so big. But then it began to make him mad. One day he looked at his garden and said, "I saw a pumpkin here last night. Why is the pumpkin not here this morning?"

The next day he said, "I thought I saw a big cucumber here. Why is it not there?"

Spider began to check his farm very carefully. He was sure there were 98 tomatoes. But when he came back, there were 95. Man, this was really getting to Spider! He told his friends that his tomatoes were missing, but they laughed at him.

"You want to tell me I'm not able to count right?" Spider asked.

Spider began to mark every single thing in his garden. Sometimes when he checked, instead of going from 1-2-3-4, the numbers went 1-3-5-7. And Spider said, "Something must be wrong!"

Spider went to Deer's hut. "Are you the one who is stealing from my garden all the time?"

Deer went: "Oh, no, no, no, no, no, no, no. Not me. You call for me every evening. You provide me dinner. Why should I go steal from your garden?"

Spider said, "I don't like stealing. I hope it's not you."

Deer said, "It's not me."

Spider went to Leopard. "Leopard, please be honest with me. Are you stealing from my garden?"

Leopard said, "No, I like meats. I really don't like too much veg-e-table. I am only eating veg-e-tables because you invite us to eat with you. You provide it for us."

Spider said, "Okay."

The vegetables kept on disappearing. Spider started to get really mad.

Spider went to Deer's house again. "Are you the one who's stealing from my garden?"

Deer said, "N-n-n-n-n-n-n-no!"

Spider said, "How come you're going 'n-n-no' like that?"

Deer said, "B-b-b-b-but that's the w-w-w-way I t-t-t-t-talk."

Spider said, "What! How come you don't talk like that all the time?"

Deer said, "When I'm m-m-m-m-mad, I t-t-t-t-talk like this." So Deer started pretending that he was mad, and that's why he was talking like this. Spider was really surprised because he never heard Deer talk like this before.

The Spider went back to Leopard's House. "Are you the one who is stealing from my garden?"

Leopard said, "I told you I like meat. I don't like veg-e-table too much. So go ask Deer."

This time when Spider came to Deer, Deer said, "Here's what you should do: Go and dig a big hole in front of the entrance to the garden, and put a lot of fire in it and build it up. Cover it with a lot of dry branches. Let the fire burn way down. When the person who is stealing from your garden goes through the entrance, they'll fall in the fire. The next day when you come, you will see them."

So Spider went and dug the hole, and lit a fire in the bottom of it. He let the fire burn way down to red-hot coals, and then he covered the hole with dry branches, just as Deer said.

But Deer knew where the hole was, because Deer was the one who told Spider the trick. So Deer went around the hole and went into Spider's garden and stole other things. Then he ran to Leopard's house, and he said, "Spider called you."

Leopard said, "Where's Spider?"

Deer said, "Spider is in his garden."

So Leopard ran to the garden. When he went through the entrance to the garden, Leopard fell in the hole. And Leopard started to get burned.

Deer ran to Spider. Deer said, "Come! Come! Come! Come! I saw the person who is stealing from the garden all the time. We should keep this old Leopard down there fighting and trying to get up."

Spider shouted to Leopard: "You've been stealing from my garden all the time! Now I've got you."

Leopard said, "I don't know what you're talking about. I just want to get out of this fire."

Spider said, "Why have you been lying to me all the time? Every time you said you are not the one. Now my trap has caught you."

Leopard said, "I don't know what you're talking about. I just want to get out of this fire."

So Leopard leaped high. Ahhh, he got out of the fire. So Leopard said, "What is all this about?"

Spider said, "Deer told me I should play this trick. And now I find out who's been stealing."

And Leopard said, "But how come Deer came to me and said that you called me to the garden?"

Spider looked at Deer and said, "Did I send you to go get Leopard?"

The Deer said, "No."

Spider said, "Ohhhh, so it's you, Deer, who's been stealing from the garden all the time."

Leopard said, "WHAT! You did that! You did this to me? Because of your trick, I've got all these black spots on my skin because I got burned in the fire!"

Since that day, all the leopards we see have black, black, black spots all over their skin.

"You did this, Deer? Because of these black spots, anywhere I see you," Leopard said, "I'M GOING TO EAT YOU!" So Deer ran away. And Leopard ran after him.

Since that day, no matter how much you train the deer, no matter how much you train the leopard, don't put them together, because Leopard is sure going to eat Deer.

That's why Deer and Leopard aren't friends now, and that's why Leopard has black spots all over his skin.

Boar Out There

Written by Cynthia Rylant   Illustrated by Fred Marvin

Everyone in Glen Morgan knew there was a wild boar in the woods over by the Miller farm. The boar was out beyond the splintery rail fence and past the old black Dodge that somehow had ended up in the woods and was missing most of its parts.

Jenny would hook her chin over the top rail of the fence, twirl a long green blade of grass in her teeth and whisper, "Boar out there."

And there were times she was sure she heard him. She imagined him running heavily through the trees, ignoring the sharp thorns and briars that raked his back and sprang away trembling.

She thought he might have a golden horn on his terrible head. The boar would run deep into the woods, then rise up on his rear hooves, throw his head toward the stars and cry a long, clear, sure note into the air. The note would glide through the night and spear the heart of the moon. The boar had no fear of the moon, Jenny knew, as she lay in bed, listening.

One hot summer day she went to find the boar. No one in Glen Morgan had ever gone past the old black Dodge and beyond, as far as she knew. But the boar was there somewhere, between those awful trees, and his dark green eyes waited for someone.

Jenny felt it was she.

Moving slowly over damp brown leaves, Jenny could sense her ears tingle and fan out as she listened for thick breathing from the trees. She stopped to pick a teaberry leaf to chew, stood a minute, then went on.

Deep in the woods she kept her eyes to the sky. She needed to be reminded that there was a world above and apart from the trees—a world of space and air, air that didn't linger all about her, didn't press deep into her skin, as forest air did.

Finally, leaning against a tree to rest, she heard him for the first time. She forgot to breathe, standing there listening to the stamping of hooves, and she choked and coughed.

Coughed!

And now the pounding was horrible, too loud and confusing for Jenny. Horrible. She stood stiff with wet eyes and knew she could always pray, but for some reason didn't.

He came through the trees so fast that she had no time to scream or run. And he was there before her.

His large gray-black body shivered as he waited just beyond the shadow of the tree she held for support. His nostrils glistened, and his eyes; but astonishingly, he was silent. He shivered and glistened and was absolutely silent.

Jenny matched his silence, and her body was rigid, but not her eyes. They traveled along his scarred, bristling back to his thick hind legs. Tears spilling and flooding her face, Jenny stared at the boar's ragged ears, caked with blood. Her tears dropped to the leaves, and the only sound between them was his slow breathing.

Then the boar snorted and jerked. But Jenny did not move.

High in the trees a bluejay yelled, and, suddenly, it was over. Jenny stood like a rock as the boar wildly flung his head and in terror bolted past her.

Past her . . .

And now, since that summer, Jenny still hooks her chin over the old rail fence, and she still whispers, "Boar out there." But when she leans on the fence, looking into the trees, her eyes are full and she leaves wet patches on the splintery wood. She is sorry for the torn ears of the boar and sorry that he has no golden horn.

But mostly she is sorry that he lives in fear of bluejays and little girls, when everyone in Glen Morgan lives in fear of him.

Spaghetti

Written by Cynthia Rylant
Illustrated by Jim McGinnis

It was evening, and people sat outside talking quietly among themselves. On the stoop of a tall building of crumbling bricks and rotting wood sat a boy. His name was Gabriel and he wished for some company.

Gabriel was thinking about things. He remembered being the only boy in class with the right answer that day, and he remembered the butter sandwich he had had for lunch. Gabriel was thinking that he would like to live outside all the time. He imagined himself carrying a pack of food and a few tools and a heavy cloth to erect a hasty tent. Gabriel saw himself sleeping among coyotes. But next he saw himself sleeping beneath the glittering lights of a movie theater, near the bus stop.

Gabriel was a boy who thought about things so seriously, so fully, that on this evening he nearly missed hearing a cry from the street. The cry was so weak and faraway in his mind that, for him, it could have been the slow lifting of a stubborn window. It could have been the creak of an old man's legs. It could have been the wind.

But it was not the wind, and it came to Gabriel slowly that he did, indeed, hear something, and that it did, indeed, sound like a cry from the street.

Gabriel picked himself up from the stoop and began to walk carefully along the edge of the street, peering into the gloom and the dusk. The cry came again and Gabriel's ears tingled and he walked faster.

He stared into the street, up and down it, knowing something was there. The street was so gray that he could not see . . . But not only the street was gray.

There, sitting on skinny stick-legs, wobbling to and fro, was a tiny gray kitten. No cars had passed to frighten it, and so it just sat in the street and cried its windy, creaky cry and waited.

Gabriel was amazed. He had never imagined he would be lucky enough one day to find a kitten. He walked into the street and lifted the kitten into his hands.

Gabriel sat on the sidewalk with the kitten next to his cheek and thought. The kitten smelled of pasta noodles, and he wondered if it belonged to a friendly Italian man somewhere in the city. Gabriel called the kitten Spaghetti.

Gabriel and Spaghetti returned to the stoop. It occurred to Gabriel to walk the neighborhood and look for the Italian man, but the purring was so loud, so near his ear, that he could not think as seriously, as fully, as before.

Gabriel no longer wanted to live outside. He knew he had a room and a bed of his own in the tall building. So he stood up, with Spaghetti under his chin, and went inside to show his kitten where they would live together.

CHARLIE BEST

Written by Ruth Corrin

Illustrated by Lesley Moyes

On Monday, Charlie Best was late for school.

"What's the story?" said Ms. Noble. "Did you forget to get out of your bed?"

"No," said Charlie. "I did not forget to get out of my bed."

"Will you look at yourself?" said Ms. Noble. "What a mess. Your socks are all muddy. And, Charlie, your knees! Oh, just look at your pants!"

Charlie Best tucked in his shirt, and thought about what to say. "Well, you see," he began, "it's like this . . .

I was tidy when I started out, and I was good
and early, too. But on the way . . . I . . . bumped
into a mountain. I really truly did! It was right in
my way, and I had to climb over it."

"Oh, yes?" said Ms. Noble, "I don't see any
mountains out there."

"It was a high mountain," said Charlie, "a
steep mountain, an awfully slippery mountain,
and there was snow on top!"

"Snow, was there?" said Ms. Noble.

"But I could only bring you a little bit," said Charlie. He could see she didn't believe him, so he scooped up a fresh lump of snow from the bottom of his schoolbag. "Snow," he said.

"Oh, Charlie," said Ms. Noble. She put the snow into an empty glass bowl on the nature table. "I see it, but I don't believe it!" she said.

"It took me such a long time to get to the top of that mountain," sighed Charlie. "That's what made me late. Luckily, it was quicker coming down. I slid down, see, on my bottom." And he bent over, and showed her the hole in his pants.

Ms. Noble did a quick bit of sewing. "No more mountains, please, Charlie," she said.

On Tuesday, the snow had melted into water, and Charlie Best was late again.

"What's the story?" said Ms. Noble. "Did you forget to get out of your bed?"

"No," said Charlie. "I did not forget to get out of my bed."

"Will you look at yourself?" said Ms. Noble. "What a mess! You're all wet, Charlie, and it isn't even raining! Oh, just look at your clothes!"

Charlie Best buttoned his shirt, and thought about what to say. "Well, you see," he began, "it's like this . . .

I was tidy when I started out, and I was good and early, too. But on the way . . . I . . . tripped into a river. I really truly did! It was right in my way, so I had to wade all the way across."

"Oh, yes?" said Ms. Noble. "I don't see any rivers out there."

"It was a green river," said Charlie, "a cold river, a wonderfully wide river, and there were twelve little red fishes swimming in it."

"Fishes, were there?" said Ms. Noble.

"But I could only bring you one," said Charlie. He could see she didn't believe him, so he reached into his rubber boot and pulled out a wriggly red fish by its tail. "Fishes," he said.

"Oh, Charlie," said Ms. Noble. She put the fish into the glass bowl with the water that used to be snow. "I see it, but I don't believe it," she said.

"It took me such a long time to get to the other side of the river," sighed Charlie. "That's what made me late. Luckily, I had my rubber boots on. Good things, rubber boots. See?"

And he emptied both his rubber boots out, right there, on the floor.

Ms. Noble handed Charlie a mop. "No more rivers, please, Charlie," she said.

On Wednesday, the fish was still swimming in the water that used to be snow, and there was Charlie Best, late again.

"What's the story?" said Ms. Noble. "Did you forget to get out of your bed?"

"No," said Charlie. "I did not forget to get out of my bed."

"Will you look at yourself?" said Ms. Noble. "What a mess! There's a bird's nest on your head. And, Charlie, your face! Oh, just look at your hair!"

Charlie Best pulled his socks up, and thought about what to say. "Well, you see," he began, "it's like this . . .

I was tidy when I started out, and I was good and early, too. But on the way . . . I . . . walked into a forest. I really truly did! It was right in my way, so I had to tramp right through it."

"Oh, yes?" said Ms. Noble. "I don't see any forests out there."

"It was a deep forest," said Charlie, " a thick forest, a particularly prickly forest, and there were twenty-nine spotted birds hiding in it."

"Birds, were there?" said Ms. Noble.

"But I could only bring you one," said Charlie. He could see she didn't believe him, so he gave a long, loud whistle, and a beautiful spotted bird flew into the room. "Birds," he said.

"Oh, Charlie," said Ms. Noble. She tried, but couldn't catch it. "I see it, but I don't believe it," she said.

"It took me such a long time to learn how to whistle like that," sighed Charlie. "That's what made me late. Luckily, I brought her nest along. It's got something in it. See?" Then Charlie Best untangled the nest from his hair. There were three spotted eggs in it.

Ms. Noble made a space for the nest on the nature table beside the fish, and the water that used to be snow. "No more forests, please, Charlie," she said.

On Thursday, the spotted bird was sitting on the eggs in her nest. And there was Charlie Best, late again.

"What's the story?" said Ms. Noble. "Did you forget to get out of your bed?"

"No," said Charlie. "I did not forget to get out of my bed."

"Will you look at yourself?" said Ms. Noble. "What a mess! You're all tangled with rope. You've lost one of your shoes. Oh, just look at your shirt!"

Charlie hitched his pants up, and thought about what to say. "Well, you see," he began, "it's like this . . .

I was tidy when I started out, and I was good and early, too. But on the way . . . I . . . fell into a cave. I really truly did! It was right in my way, so I had to be very brave and grope my way through it."

"Oh, yes?" said Ms. Noble. "I don't see any caves out there."

"It was a huge cave," said Charlie, "a damp cave, a dreadfully dark cave, and there were thirty-two dragons roaring in it!"

"Dragons, were there?" said Ms. Noble.

"But I could only bring you one," said Charlie, though he could see she didn't believe him.

"I don't see any dragon, " said Ms. Noble, and winked at the other children. "Is it in your school bag?"

"It was a yellow dragon," said Charlie, "a bellowing dragon, and it licked me all over."

"Yellow, was it?" Ms. Noble looked under Charlie's hat. "I don't see any dragon," she said.

"It was a rumbly dragon," said Charlie, "a loud dragon, a horribly hot dragon, and it breathed green steam."

"Breathed steam, did it?" said Ms. Noble. "I don't see any dragon. Is it in your pocket?"

The other children were jumping up and down. Ms. Noble held her sides and laughed and laughed, the spotted bird whistled, and the wriggly fish swam round and round and round in the water that used to be snow.

"It took me such a long time to get out of that cave," said Charlie.

Ms. Noble's sides were sore from so much laughing. "Well, it would," she said, "especially with a dragon! I suppose that's what made you late."

"Right," said Charlie. "Luckily, I had this rope with me. You need a rope when you've got a dragon to catch. Don't you agree?"

Then Charlie Best took hold of his tangled rope, and pulled.

The other children stopped jumping up and down.
Ms. Noble stopped laughing, and took two steps backward.
The spotted bird stopped whistling, and the wriggly red fish
stopped swimming round and round in the water that used
to be snow.

"Oh, Charlie," whispered Ms. Noble.
"I see, but I don't believe it!"
Then everyone was quiet.

Tied to the other end of Charlie Best's rope was a rumbly, yellow dragon!

Ms. Noble sat down. "No more caves, please, Charlie," she said.

On Friday, the spotted bird was still there on her nest, and the fish was still swimming in the water that used to be snow. And Charlie Best was the first kid at school. He had his dragon with him.

"I see it, but I don't believe it," said Ms. Noble. She wasn't looking at the dragon; she was looking at Charlie. "Will you look at yourself?" she said. "You're tidy!"

Charlie looked down at his clothes. Even his shirt was tucked in.

"What's the story, Charlie Best? Couldn't you find any caves today? No rivers to wade? No forests to tramp? Not even a mountain to climb?"

The dragon yawned a yellow yawn, and let out a cloud of green steam. Ms. Noble opened the window.

Charlie was embarrassed. "Well, you see," he began, "it's like this . . .

I was tidy when I started out, and I was good and early, too . . ."

"That's what I like to see, Charlie," said Ms. Noble, and the dragon gave him a hot, yellow lick.

"But I didn't want to be early," said Charlie, "and I tried to get my clothes messed up, I really truly did. All I needed was a cave, or a river to cross, or a forest, or even a mountain to climb. I wanted to do all those things. But . . . and it's not fair . . .

my dragon wouldn't let me!"

The Pancake Collector

by Jack Prelutsky

Come visit my pancake collection,
it's unique in the civilized world.
I have pancakes of every description,
pancakes flaky and fluffy and curled.

I have pancakes of various sizes,
pancakes regular, heavy and light,
underdone pancakes and overdone pancakes,
and pancakes done perfectly right.

I have pancakes locked up in the closets,
I have pancakes on hangers and hooks.
They're in bags and in boxes and bureaus,
and pressed in the pages of books.

There are pretty ones sewn to the cushions
and tastefully pinned to the drapes.
The ceilings are coated with pancakes,
and the carpets are covered with crepes.

I have pancakes in most of my pockets,
and concealed in the linings of suits.
There are tiny ones stuffed in my mittens
and larger ones packed in my boots.

I have extras of most of my pancakes,
I maintain them in rows on these shelves,
and if you say nice things about them,
you may take a few home for yourselves.

I see that you've got to be going,
Won't you let yourselves out by the door?
It is time that I pour out the batter
and bake up a few hundred more.

NOT JUST ANY RING

by Danita Ross Haller

pictures by Deborah Kogan Ray

Jessie Yano wants a ring.
But not just any ring.

Jessie Yano wants a ring
like Nellie Sena's.
Nellie Sena's ring is silver
with a smooth, flat,
polished black stone.
And in the center
of the stone
there is a tiny silver dove.
So tiny
almost no one notices.
But Jessie Yano notices.

And Jessie Yano knows
something else
about that ring.
She knows it is a magic ring.
When Nellie Sena
wears that silver ring,
she has good days.

Nellie Sena told her about that ring—
how it came from the mission shop,
and how an old man in a long brown robe
blessed it.
That's why the ring brings good days for her.

Today everything was wrong
for Jessie Yano.
Now as she walks the mesa path
to her home,
she wishes like anything
for a silver ring
with a black stone
and a tiny silver dove.
She holds her hands out in front of her
and imagines that ring
on her finger.
She knows how good it would feel
and how proud she would be
to have her own silver ring.

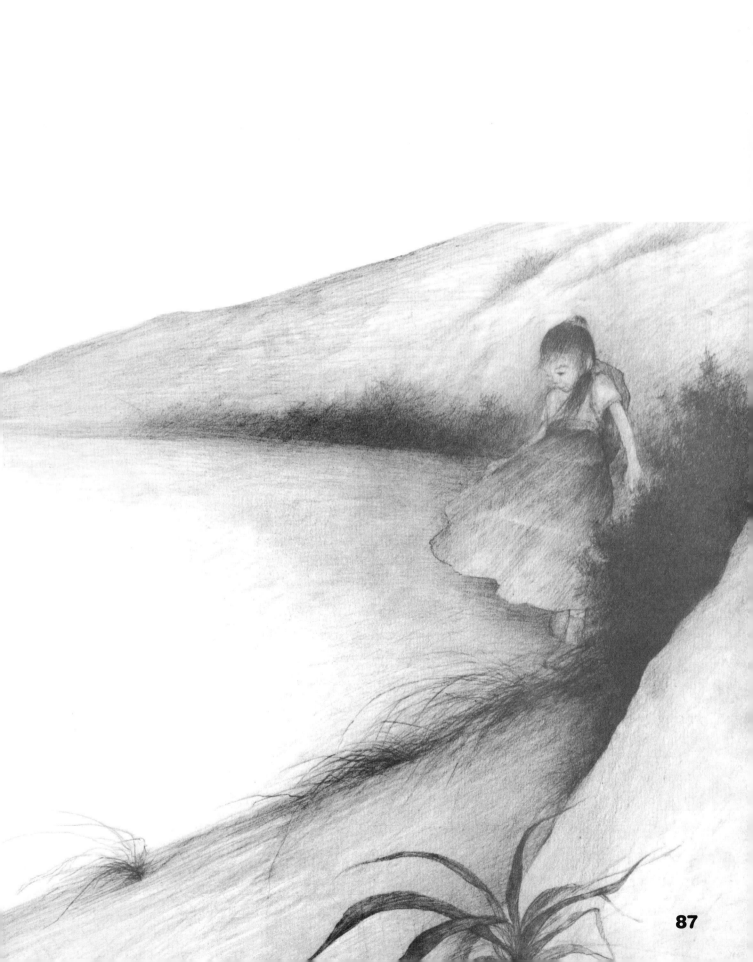

Jessie Yano's grandfather
sits by the path
waiting for Jessie.
She sees him now;
sees his green flannel shirt
and a green flannel arm
waving high in the air.
She hurries to meet him.

Jessie sits awhile
by her grandfather.
They talk of the day.

Grandfather tells
of the sculpture he works at.
Slowly, slowly
in his workshop
every day,
he chips away at stone.
One day,
when he has chipped away enough,
the block of stone
will be a beautiful face.

Jessie looks at her grandfather's hands.
Strong hands, skilled hands.
She tries to imagine
that silver ring
on those fingers,
but can't.

Now she speaks of what is on her mind,
the only thing that is on her mind.
"Grandfather, I need a ring.
I need a silver ring like Nellie Sena's,
a silver ring to bring good days."
"And does Nellie Sena's silver ring
bring her good days?"

"Yes, Grandfather,
it always brings her good days.
The ring came from the mission shop.
It was blessed
especially to bring good days."

"Ahhh." Grandfather nods;
his eyes look far away.
No more is said about the ring this day.

But Jessie Yano
does not forget the silver ring.
She cannot forget it.

She makes paper rings
and clay rings
and ribbon rings.
But they are not
that silver ring.
It's that silver ring she needs.

One day
as Jessie walks the worn path home,
her grandfather waits for her
in the white pickup truck.
He motions for Jessie to get in.
"Where are we going?" Jessie asks.
"It is a surprise, Jessie.
A surprise for you."

They drive slowly
down off the mesa
and into the desert country.
The road winds
and twists
and turns
for some time.

At last
Jessie sees
the old brown mission church.
She looks at her grandfather.
He smiles,
and Jessie hopes she is right
about this surprise.

Jessie Yano and her grandfather
walk together
to the door of a small shop
at the side of the mission church.
Little glass chimes tinkle
as the wooden door opens.

Inside it is dim and cool
and smells of candles and
earthen walls.
Jessie sees shelves
of colorful statues
and vases.

Then she sees a glass counter.
And behind the glass,
on the top shelf,
she sees the rings.

"Here, Grandfather,
here they are," Jessie whispers excitedly.
A lady with a kind face
slides back the glass door
and takes out the tray.
There are many different rings.
Jessie looks up one row
and down another.
Finally
Jessie sees
one silver ring
with a smooth, flat,
polished black stone.
In the center of the stone
there is a tiny silver dove.

Jessie lifts the ring
out of the tray
and slides it onto her finger.
It is beautiful.

She looks at her grandfather.
He nods his head yes.
It is hers.

Jessie stops as they walk out
toward the truck.
"Grandfather, I need my ring blessed."
"I don't believe there is anyone here
to bless it today, Jessie."
"But it must be blessed!
Can't you bless it, Grandfather?"

Grandfather stoops down
and takes her hands in his.
"I cannot bless your ring, Jessie,
but together we might make a prayer
for the ring and for good days."

"Yes, I would like that," says Jessie.

"Jessie, before we make a prayer
I must say some things to you of magic
and of good days.

When I take a stone and shape it
into a deer, or a bird, or a face,
you often say
that my hands must be magic.
I say to you now, Jessie,
that my hands are my tools,
only my tools.
Any magic is within my heart.
If you believe in something
with your heart,
then it can be yours.
If you believe this will be
a good ring for you,
then it will be.
If you believe in good days,
then they will come.
Always,
the real magic
is within your heart."

Jessie Yano sits beside her grandfather
on an old wooden bench
outside the mission church.

Together
they make a prayer for the ring
and for good days.
Then they drive toward home.

The old truck comes to the fork
in the road at the bottom of the great mesa.
To the left
the road climbs slowly until it becomes
a rim on the side of the mesa.
This is the road everyone travels.

To the right
the road veers off into the canyon
and wanders for some miles
before climbing the mesa.
This is the old road, a longer trip
and difficult in some places.
But it is beautiful in the canyon,
especially at sunset.
This is the road
Jessie and her grandfather like the best.
She is glad
when the truck turns to the right,
into the canyon.

The old dirt road
is rutted and bumpy.
But Jessie does not mind.
She sees only the setting sun,
thinks only of her silver ring.

The white truck comes to a sudden stop.
Directly in front of them
the road dips into a sandy arroyo.
The sand will be soft this time of year,
and Grandfather is not certain
the truck can make it across.
"We can make it, Grandfather,
sure we can," Jessie says.
Grandfather backs the truck down the road
and then starts forward as fast as he can.
They hit the arroyo.
The wheels slide,
then straighten and race forward.
Suddenly, the back tires spin,
and the truck stops.
Grandfather and Jessie climb out
to have a look.
The wheels are buried in the sand.
"We are certainly stuck," Grandfather says.
Grandfather's face is serious
as he looks at the sky.
The sun is sinking low.

"Jessie, soon it will be dark.
It is several miles back to the other road,
and several miles ahead to where this road
climbs out of the canyon.
I believe the shortest route
to the top of the mesa
is straight up the side."
Jessie looks up the side
of the great mesa.
It is a long way to the top.

"Jessie, I want you to wait in the truck
where you will be warm and safe
until I get back with help."

"No, Grandfather.
If you are going to climb the mesa,
then I will climb the mesa too.
I am strong,
and besides, I have my silver ring.
It is time for it to bring us good luck."

Together they start
up the side of the great mesa.
It is difficult to climb.
Rocks and boulders jut out everywhere.
Several times Jessie slips.
Then Grandfather slips.
Only one time, but it is a bad slip.
Grandfather's ankle turns and twists.
He drops to his knees in pain.

They examine the ankle.
It is already starting to swell.
Grandfather tries to stand, but can't.
It is too painful.
He sits, resting his head in his hands.
Jessie stands very still.
Fear crawls slowly up her body,
making her shiver.

Finally Grandfather speaks.
"Jessie, now you must be a mountain goat.
Take your magic ring
and climb to the top of the mesa for help."

Jessie looks at her grandfather.
Tears blur her eyes.
"Grandfather, I can't leave you here alone."

"Jessie, I will be fine. Remember,
I am quite at home
among these rocks and stones.
You must go and get help
while there is still light."

Jessie's heart pounds hard against her chest.
How can these things happen
now that she has her silver ring?
She looks at the ring.
"This is not a magic ring.
It is not even a good ring.
I hate it!"
She pulls the ring off her finger
and throws it to the ground.

Jessie clings to her grandfather
for a moment
and then begins the long climb
up the mesa.

Looking up,
Jessie picks out a lone juniper tree
at the very top of the mesa.
She will not lose sight of that tree.
She will touch that tree.

Stumbling now,
she plunges forward.
Dried brush scratches at her legs
and snags her clothing.
Rocks slip beneath her feet.
Still she pushes upward,
watching that tree.
Soon she is breathing hard and fast.
Her throat is dry.
The mesa seems to swallow her,
but the tree is closer, a little closer.

Jessie moves on,
crawling and climbing the mesa
like a little worm.

The mesa stands above her
like a wall.
This is the steepest part of the climb,
and the sandy soil
makes it hard to get a good hold.
Small trees grow straight out into the air.
The first one Jessie reaches for
comes out by its roots.
Jessie slides down, down,
until she catches herself on a vine.
She clings there,
against the side of the mesa,
her body shaking,
her fingers and feet dug into the earth.

She closes her eyes.
She cannot move even one more inch.
She thinks she may die
right there on the side of the mesa.
Then she opens her eyes
and sees her hands.
She wishes now that she had the silver ring.
She wishes she had given it one more chance.
She wishes she had even a little magic.
Jessie remembers her grandfather
somewhere below her, waiting.
She remembers about the magic in his heart.
She hears his words about believing with your heart.
But all her heart can do is pound.

She thinks of her grandfather's strong hands.
She is his granddaughter.
She has strong hands too.
Suddenly she wants her hands to work,
to pull her up,
up to the top of the mesa.
She wants it more than anything in the world.
She watches her hands.
They are moving, reaching, grabbing,
digging into the earth.
Her feet follow,
digging, pushing, climbing.

She talks to the mesa.
Talks to the trees.
Talks to anything that might hear her
as she scrambles and slides and reaches
and finally pulls herself to the top
of the great mesa.

Jessie Yano lies exhausted
on the flat earth of the mesa top—
but only for a moment.
Then she jumps up.

The sun has set.
She cannot see the truck
or her grandfather
down in the canyon.
But she waves a juniper limb
and hollers that she is safe.
Then she runs toward the lights of houses
that dot the mesa.
She runs for help.

Much later,
riding in a truck,
Jessie Yano arrives back in the canyon
with friends.
She sees her grandfather
sitting near his truck
by a small fire.
Jessie runs to him
and throws both arms around him.

"Grandfather, how did you get back down here?"
"I made a staff out of a tree limb
and managed to scoot back down.
But it is not so special that I made it
to the bottom of the mesa, Jessie.
What is special
is that you made it to the top."

Jessie Yano looks up at the mesa.
Even in the darkness
its great shape
looms toward the sky.
She had climbed it all right.
She guesses
she had some of that magic
after all.
The real magic
that is in the heart.

"Jessie," Grandfather speaks softly.
"I have something for you."
He opens his hands.
There, in the palm of one hand,
is the silver ring.

Jessie takes the ring
and slides it back onto her finger.
She thinks of how good it feels.
Now she watches
as the white truck is towed out of the arroyo.
Suddenly
she feels very happy
about this day.

It has been a good day after all.

A Lucky Thing

by Alice Schertle

High
up in a hawthorn tree
a robin perched, where he could see
into a coop of wire and wood.
Inside the coop a farmer stood
flinging grain upon the ground.
Twelve fat chickens gathered round.

The robin,
singing, cocked his head
and watched the chickens being fed.
He saw it was a lucky thing
to be a chicken: Farmers bring
you golden grain, scoop after scoop,
if you're a chicken in a coop—
a lovely coop with nesting boxes
safe from cats and crows and foxes.

The chickens
in the coop could see
the bird. They heard his melody
and clucked it was a lucky thing
to be a robin who could sing
a song upon a hawthorn tree.
They watched him through the woven wire.
They saw him fly up high, and higher.

Twelve fat chickens
scratched the floor.
The farmer closed
and latched
the door.

The New Kid

by Mike Makley

Our baseball team never did very much,
we had me and PeeWee and Earl and Dutch.
And the Oak Street Tigers always got beat
until the new kid moved in on our street.

The kid moved in with a mitt and a bat
and an official New York Yankee hat.
The new kid plays shortstop or second base
and can outrun us all in any place.

The kid never muffs a grounder or fly
no matter how hard it's hit or how high.
And the new kid always acts quite polite,
never yelling or spitting or starting a fight.

We were playing the league champs just last week;
they were trying to break our winning streak.
In the last inning the score was one–one,
when the new kid swung and hit a home run.

A few of the kids and their parents say
they don't believe that the new kid should play.
But she's good as me, Dutch, PeeWee, or Earl,
so we don't care that the new kid's a girl.

Steps

by Deborah M. Newton Chocolate
Illustrated by Morissa Lipstein

"Somebody has to take the first step," said Sonny and Jamal's mother.

"Your Mama's right," said their father. But the two nine-year-old boys sat quietly, staring at each other. They were new stepbrothers.

"Okay, boys," said their father. "Your mother and I still have boxes to unpack. So while we're doing that, why don't you two spend some time getting to know each other better."

"But, Dad," groaned Jamal, jumping up from his bed, "I have baseball practice."

"Mama?" whined Sonny.

"Family is a lot more important than baseball," said their mother, as both parents left the room.

When the door was closed, Jamal threw himself on the bed. "I wish you would've never come here to live!" he said.

"I wish I didn't live here, either," Sonny shot back at him. He looked around and quickly decided that Jamal's room wasn't big enough for the two of them to share.

"Well, that's one thing we both agree on," said Jamal.

"What's that?" Sonny said.

"We both wish you'd never have come here!"

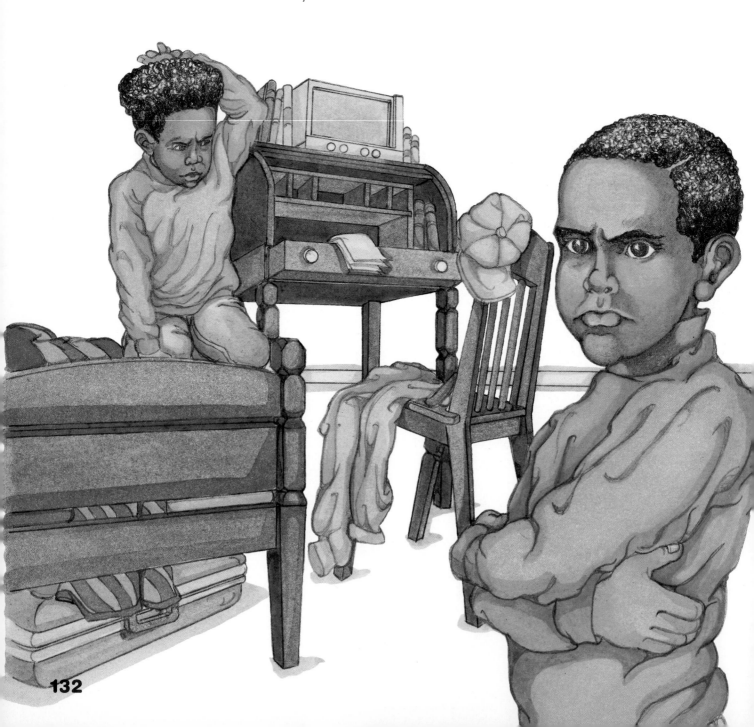

Later that evening, Jamal's father began unpacking a big sewing machine from a heavy wooden crate.

"Look!" said Sonny, pointing to a leg on a sewing machine. "That leg is loose. One of the screws must have fallen out again."

Jamal and his father knelt down beside the sewing machine and looked underneath. "You're right," said their father. "But how did you know a screw was missing?"

"That screw was always falling out at Grandma's house," explained Sonny. "Every time Grandma got in the mood to clean, Grandpa and I had to move this old machine from room to room. And that screw was always falling out."

"Well, if the machine is that old," cracked Jamal, "why don't you just throw it out and buy a new one?"

Sonny took a deep breath. He could feel his ears turning hot, the way they always did when he was angry.

Their father put his hands on Sonny's shoulders. "Take it easy, son," he said. And then he turned to Jamal.

"Listen to me, Jamal," said their father. "Sonny is your stepbrother. And while this sewing machine may seem old to you, it means a lot to Sonny."

Jamal didn't say anything, but he didn't like the way his father was taking Sonny's side.

"In the morning," their dad said, I want you both to go to the hardware store. We'll buy some screws and fix up this sewing machine like new for your mother."

"Aw, no!" complained Jamal. "First no baseball, and now this!"

Later, in bed that night, Jamal couldn't help thinking about how his father had stood up for Sonny. Sonny was putting his pajamas on now. When he finished, he crossed the room and opened the window.

"What do you think you're doing?" Jamal asked.

"What does it look like I'm doing?" Sonny said. "I'm opening the window."

"Let's get one thing straight," said Jamal, getting up from his bed. "This is my side of the room. And, this is my hockey stick," he said, picking up his stick. "And, this is my baseball mitt. Get it?"

Sonny just looked at Jamal. Then, he climbed into bed and turned his back on his stepbrother.

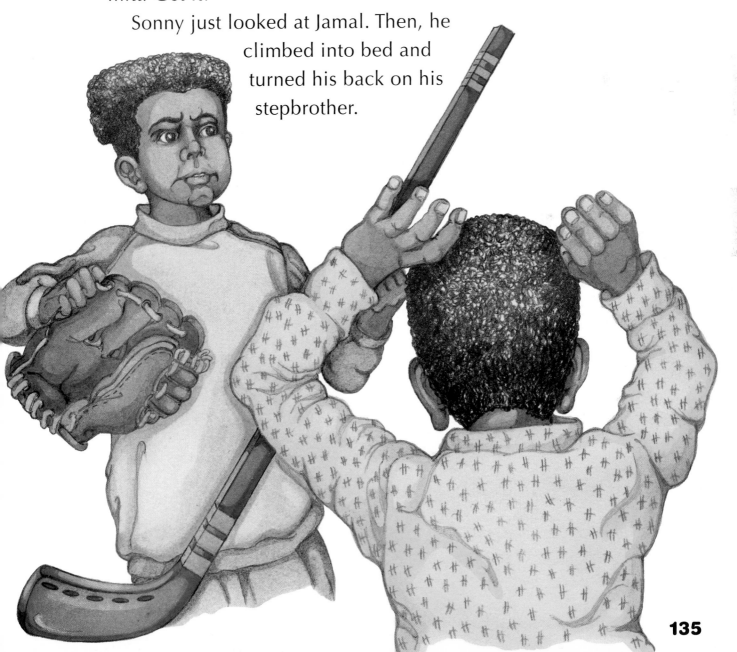

The next day, after breakfast, the two boys grabbed their bicycles and started out for the hardware store. Jamal knew the neighborhood better, so he sped through the streets. It was hard for Sonny to keep up with him. And, to make matters worse, Jamal kept confusing Sonny by darting in and out of narrow side streets.

Before long, they came to a vacant lot where Jamal stopped to catch his breath. The lot was covered with huge sand hills.

With a mean smile on his face, Jamal said to Sonny, "Let's ride some hills."

"I don't think we should," said Sonny.

"You're not chicken, are you," Jamal asked. He began to tease Sonny. "Here chick, chick, chick, chick, chick!" he said. Sonny could feel his ears turning hot again.

"Come on, Sonny!" Jamal dared. "One ride won't hurt."

Sonny didn't want Jamal to know that he had broken his arm once, riding on a dirt hill.

"Come on," shouted Jamal, racing towards the tallest hill. "Come on," he yelled over his shoulder. "I'll even go first."

Before Sonny could say anything, Jamal had reached the hill and was already climbing fast.

Suddenly Sonny saw Jamal flying head first down a steep bank of the hill. Without thinking, Sonny pedaled as hard as he could until he reached the bottom of the hill where his stepbrother lay.

"Owwwww!" moaned Jamal. "My leg!" he cried. "I think it's broken."

Sonny leaped off his bike. He tried to help Jamal get on his feet.

"Get up," pleaded Sonny.

Jamal's leg hurt so badly, he felt like crying. But he wouldn't cry—not in front of Sonny.

"Never mind. Don't move anymore," said Sonny. "I don't want to leave you here alone, but I have to go get help."

Both boys became quiet. Sonny quickly scanned the area around the vacant lot. There was a small grocery store on the corner. He could get help there.

Jamal began to look scared, and Sonny knew that his leg must really hurt. Sonny knelt down beside Jamal and looked straight into his eyes. When he spoke, his voice was a lot calmer than he felt.

"I'm going to the store to get help. Just rest on the ground and don't move. I'll be back as soon as I can."

Jamal didn't say anything, but he lay back obediently and prepared to wait. Sonny got on his bike and sped off toward the store.

The next hour was kind of a blur to Sonny. Two phone calls from the grocery store brought their parents and an Emergency Squad to the vacant lot. The next thing Sonny knew, they were all on their way to a hospital.

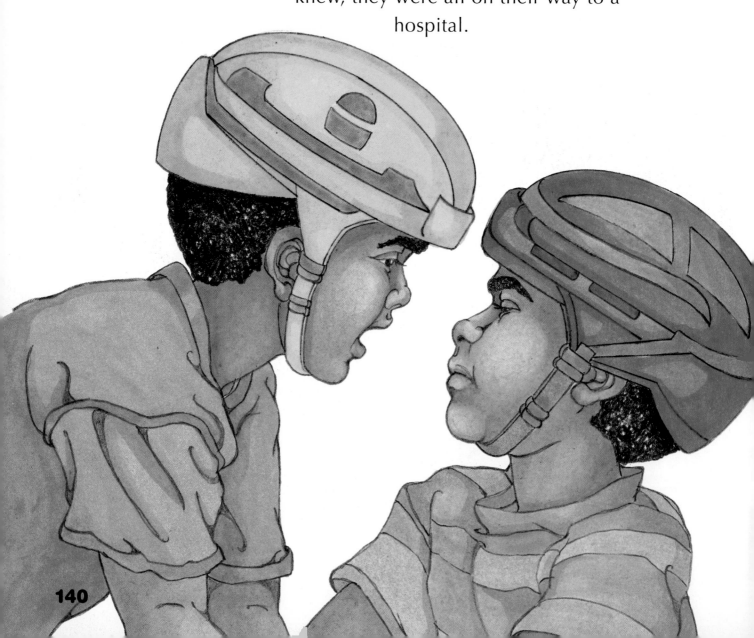

At the hospital, the doctor told them, "That broken leg means no more baseball this summer."

Sonny sat at his stepbrother's bedside and saw the disappointment in his face.

Suddenly, Sonny heard himself saying, "I'll help you keep your pitching arm in shape." And then he smiled and said, "For that you won't need legs."

Jamal looked at Sonny. And, for the first time, he felt sure that they could be not only stepbrothers, but friends.

"You know?" said Jamal. "For a stepbrother, you're not half bad!"

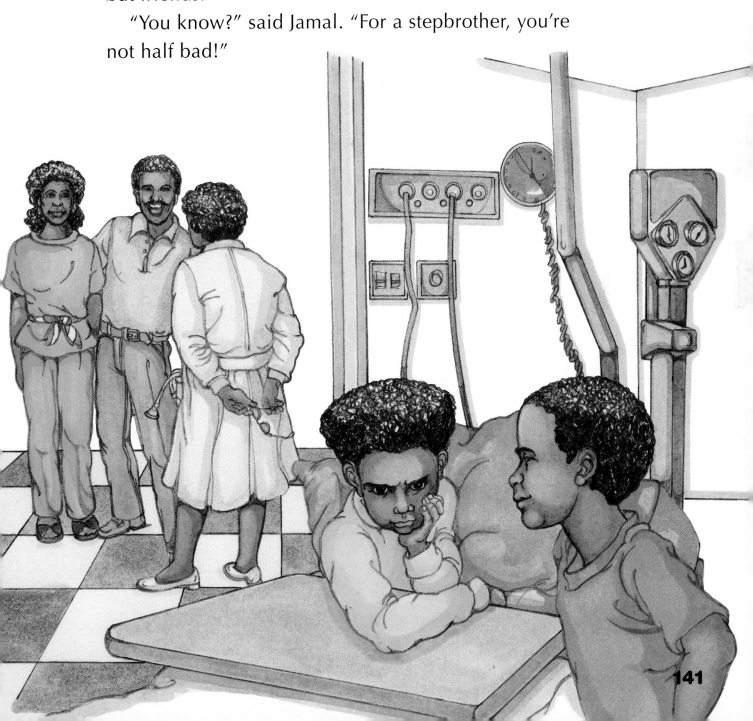

The next afternoon, Sonny and Jamal were sitting on the
front porch. They heard someone calling Jamal's name.

"Hey, Jamal!" came a voice from across the yard. It was
his next-door neighbor Rudy, who had been away on
vacation all summer.

"I heard about your leg," Rudy said. "That's a swell cast,"
he said when he came closer. "May I sign it?"

"Sure," said Jamal, handing him some colored markers.

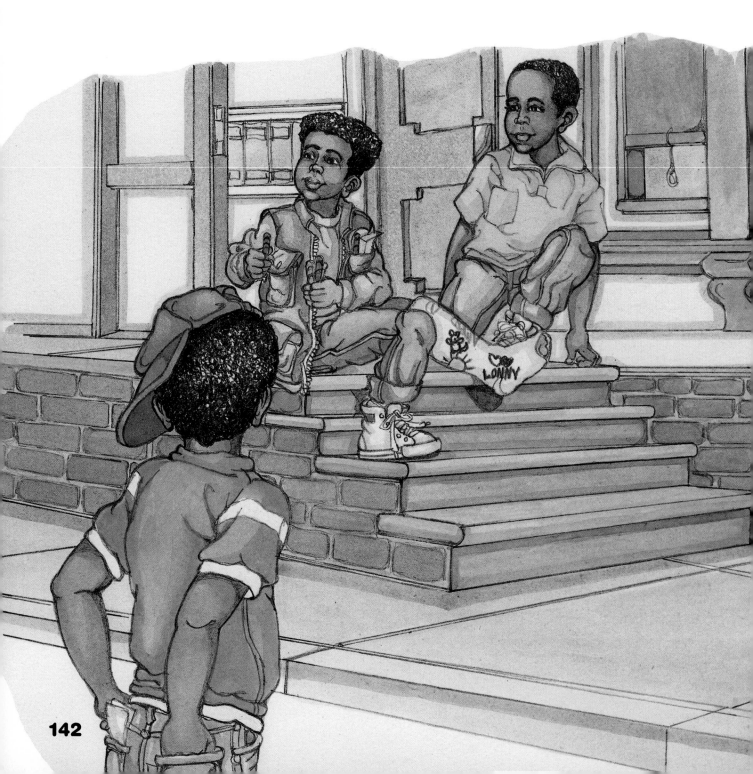

"Hi!" said Rudy to Sonny, noticing him for the very first time.

"Hi!" said Sonny.

"Is he your cousin, Jamal?" Rudy asked. Rudy was bent over Jamal's cast, writing his name in bright neon colors. Jamal and Sonny looked at each other and laughed.

"Naw," answered Jamal. "He's not my cousin." Smiling, Jamal said proudly, "Rudy, meet Sonny—my new step!"

The Soup Stone

A Belgian folk tale retold by Maria Leach
Illustrated by Karen Bauman

One day a soldier was walking home from the wars and came to a village. The wind was cold; the sky was gray, and the soldier was hungry. He stopped at a house on the edge of the village and asked for something to eat. "We have nothing for ourselves," the people said, so the soldier went on.

He stopped at the next house and asked for something to eat. "We have nothing for ourselves," the people said.

"Have you got a big pot?" the soldier asked. Yes, they had a big iron pot.

"Have you got water?" he asked. Yes, they had plenty of water.

"Fill the pot with water and put it on the fire," the soldier said, "for I have a soup stone with me."

"A soup stone?" they asked. "What is that?"

"It is a stone that makes soup," the soldier replied. And they all gathered round to see this wonder.

The woman of the house filled the big pot with water and hung it over the fire. The soldier took a stone from his pocket (it looked like any stone a man might pick up on the road) and tossed it into the pot. "Now let it boil," he said. So they all sat down to wait for the pot to boil.

"Could you spare a bit of salt for it?" the soldier asked.

"Of course," the woman said, and she pulled out the salt box. The soldier took a fistful of salt and threw it in, for it was a big pot. Then they all sat back to wait.

"A few carrots would taste good in it," the soldier said longingly.

"Oh, we have a few carrots," the woman said, and she pulled them out from under a bench, where the soldier had been eyeing them. So they threw in the carrots. And while the carrots boiled, the soldier told them stories of his adventures.

"A few potatoes would be good, wouldn't they?" the soldier said. "They'd thicken the soup a bit."

"We have a few potatoes," said the oldest girl. "I'll get them." So they put the potatoes in the pot and waited for the soup to boil.

"An onion does give a good flavor," the soldier said.

"Run next door and ask the neighbor for an onion," the farmer told his smallest son. The child ran out of the house and came back with three onions. So they put the onions in. While they were waiting, they were cracking jokes and telling tales.

". . . And I haven't tasted cabbage since I left my mother's house" the soldier was saying. "Run out into the garden and pull a cabbage," said the mother. And a small girl ran out and came back with a cabbage. And they put that in.

"It won't be long now," the soldier said.

"Just a little longer," the woman said, stirring the pot with a long ladle.

At that moment the oldest son came in. He had
been hunting and brought home two rabbits.

"Just what we need for the finishing touch!" cried
the soldier, and it was only a matter of minutes before
the rabbits were cut up and thrown into the pot.

"Ha!" said the hungry hunter. "The smell of a
fine soup."

"The traveler has brought a soup stone," the farmer
said to his son, "and he is making soup with it in the
pot."

At last the soup was ready, and it was good. There was enough for all: the soldier and the farmer and his wife, the oldest girl and the oldest son, the little girl, and the little son.

"It's a wonderful soup," the farmer said.

"It's a wonderful stone," the wife said.

"It is," the soldier said, "and it will make soup forever if you follow the formula we used today."

So they finished the soup. And when the soldier said good-bye, he gave the woman the stone to pay back the kindness. She protested politely.

"It's nothing," the soldier said and went on his way without the stone.

Luckily, he found another just before he came to the next village.

Amelia Bedelia

by Peggy Parish
Pictures by Fritz Siebel

"Oh, Amelia Bedelia, your first day of work,
and I can't be here. But I made a list for you.
You do just what the list says," said Mrs. Rogers.

Mrs. Rogers got into the car with Mr. Rogers.
They drove away.

"My, what nice folks. I'm going to like
working here," said Amelia Bedelia.

Amelia Bedelia went inside. "Such a grand house. These must be rich folks. But I must get to work. Here I stand just looking. And me with a whole list of things to do."

Amelia Bedelia stood there a minute longer.

"I think I'll make a surprise for them. I'll make lemon-meringue pie. I do make good pies."

So Amelia Bedelia went into the kitchen. She put a little of this and a pinch of that into a bowl. She mixed and she rolled.

Soon her pie was ready to go into the oven.
"There," said Amelia Bedelia. "That's done."

"Now let's see what this list says."
Amelia Bedelia read,

Change the towels in the green bathroom.

Amelia Bedelia found the green bathroom.
"Those towels are very nice. Why change them?"
she thought.

Then Amelia Bedelia remembered what Mrs. Rogers had said. She must do just what the list told her.

"Well, all right," said Amelia Bedelia. Amelia Bedelia got some scissors. She snipped a little here and a little there. And she changed those towels.

"There," said Amelia Bedelia. She looked at
her list again.

Dust the furniture.

"Did you ever hear tell of such a silly thing.
At my house we undust the furniture. But to
each his own way."

Amelia Bedelia took one last look at
the bathroom. She saw a big box with
the words *Dusting Powder* on it.

"Well, look at that. A special powder to dust with!" exclaimed Amelia Bedelia. So Amelia Bedelia dusted the furniture.

"That should be dusty enough. My, how nice it smells."

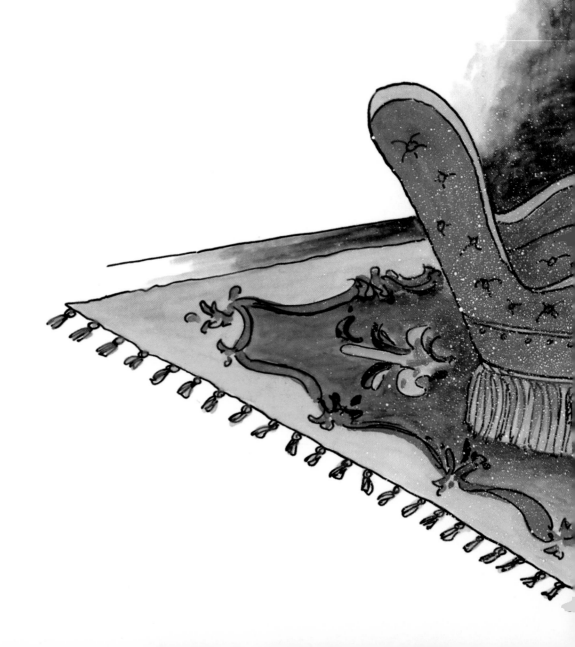

Draw the drapes when the sun comes in.

read Amelia Bedelia. She looked up. The sun was coming in. Amelia Bedelia looked at the list again.

"Draw the drapes? That's what it says. I'm not much of a hand at drawing, but I'll try."

So Amelia Bedelia sat right down and
she drew those drapes.

Amelia Bedelia marked off about the drapes.
"Now what?"

Put the lights out when you finish in the living room.

Amelia Bedelia thought about this a minute.
She switched off the lights. Then she carefully
unscrewed each bulb.

And Amelia Bedelia put the lights out. "So those things need to be aired out, too. Just like pillows and babies. Oh, I do have a lot to learn."

"My pie!" exclaimed Amelia Bedelia.
She hurried to the kitchen.

"Just right," she said. She took the pie
out of the oven and put it on the table to
cool. Then she looked at the list.

Measure two cups of rice.

"That's next," said Amelia Bedelia.

Amelia Bedelia found two cups. She filled them with rice.

And Amelia Bedelia measured that rice.

Amelia Bedelia laughed.
"These folks do want me to do funny things."
Then she poured the rice back into the container.

The meat market will deliver a steak and a chicken.

Please trim the fat before you put the steak in the icebox.

And please dress the chicken.

When the meat arrived, Amelia Bedelia
opened the bag. She looked at the steak for
a long time.

"Yes," she said. "That will do nicely."

Amelia Bedelia got some lace and bits of ribbon. And Amelia Bedelia trimmed that fat before she put the steak in the icebox.

"Now I must dress the chicken. I wonder if she wants a he chicken or a she chicken?" said Amelia Bedelia. Amelia Bedelia went right to work. Soon the chicken was finished.

Amelia Bedelia heard the door open.
"The folks are back," she said. She rushed
out to meet them.

"Amelia Bedelia, why are all the light bulbs outside?" asked Mr. Rogers.

"The list just said to put the lights
out," said Amelia Bedelia. "It didn't say to
bring them back in. Oh, I do hope they
didn't get aired too long."

"Amelia Bedelia, the sun will fade the furniture. I asked you to draw the drapes," said Mrs. Rogers.
"I did! I did! See," said Amelia Bedelia.
She held up her picture.

Then Mrs. Rogers saw the furniture.
"The furniture!" she cried.

"Did I dust it well enough?"
asked Amelia Bedelia. "That's such
nice dusting powder."

Mr. Rogers went to wash his hands.
"I say," he called. "These are very
unusual towels."

Mrs. Rogers dashed into the bathroom.
"Oh, my best towels," she said.
"Didn't I change them enough?"
asked Amelia Bedelia.

Mrs. Rogers went to the kitchen.
"I'll cook the dinner. Where is the
rice I asked you to measure?"

"I put it back in the container. But
I remember—it measured four and a half inches,"
said Amelia Bedelia.

"Was the meat delivered?" asked Mrs. Rogers.

"Yes," said Amelia Bedelia. "I trimmed the fat just like you said. It does look nice."

Mrs. Rogers rushed to the icebox. She opened it.

"Lace! Ribbons! Oh, dear!" said Mrs. Rogers.

"The chicken—you dressed the chicken?" asked
Mrs. Rogers.

"Yes, and I found the nicest box to put him
in," said Amelia Bedelia.

"Box!" exclaimed Mrs. Rogers. Mrs. Rogers
hurried over to the box. She lifted the lid.
There lay the chicken. And he
was just as dressed as he could be.

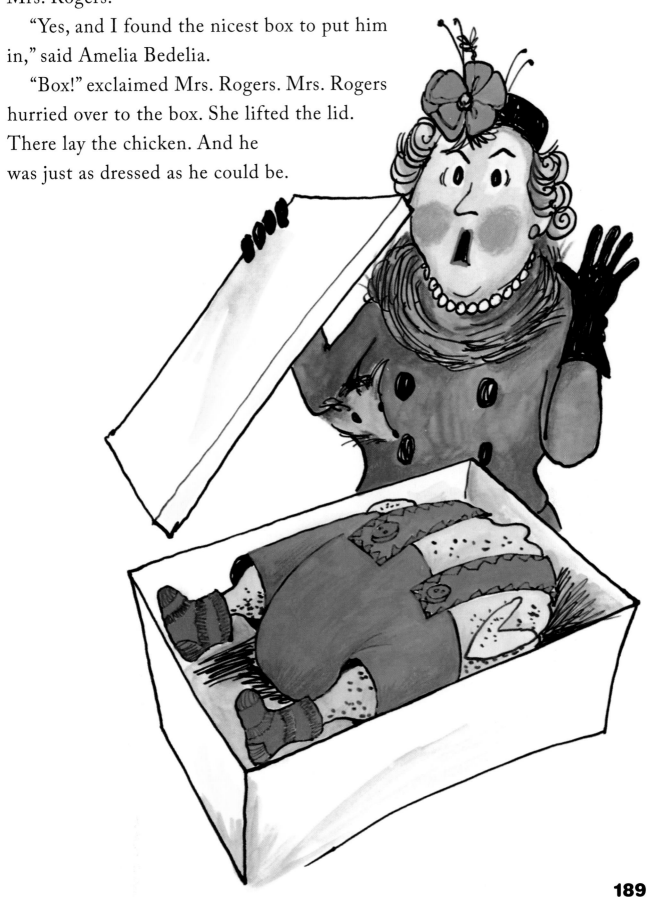

Mrs. Rogers was angry. She was very angry. She opened her mouth. Mrs. Rogers meant to tell Amelia Bedelia she was fired. But before she could get the words out, Mr. Rogers put something in her mouth. It was so good Mrs. Rogers forgot about being angry.

"Lemon-meringue pie!" she exclaimed.

"I made it to surprise you," said Amelia Bedelia happily.

So right then and there Mr. and Mrs. Rogers decided that Amelia Bedelia must stay. And so she did. Mrs. Rogers learned to say undust the furniture, unlight the lights, close the drapes, and things liked that.

Mr. Rogers didn't care if Amelia Bedelia trimmed all his steaks with lace.

All he cared about was having her there to make lemon-meringue pie.

My (Wow!) Summer VACATION

by Susan Cornell Poskanzer

Illustrated by Meryl Henderson

I'd heard about the rattlesnakes. I'd heard about the scorpions. I'd heard about the red fire ants whose bites make your skin think it's in flames. So when Mom asked me, "How'd you like to raft down the Colorado River for eight days through the Grand Canyon in Arizona?" you can imagine what I said.

"What's wrong with staying in New Jersey?" I answered. "My friends are here. And there are no rattlesnakes, scorpions, or fire ants."

"Don't be silly," Mom said. "You'll have a great time."

That's how I found myself in the middle of the huge rocky cliffs called the Grand Canyon.

I was the only kid on our raft, a rubber contraption with a motor, giant pontoons, four big supply boxes, and 16 people. Our guides, Owen and P.J., were comforting from the start of the trip at Lee's Ferry.

"We shouldn't see more than a dozen or so rattlesnakes," joked Owen.

"It's the height of lizard season, especially gila monsters," said P.J. flashing me a smile.

I pretended to ignore him. I didn't think much of this trip from the start. In fact, I had just three little goals. I wrote them on the back of our guidebook.

MY GOALS FOR THIS TRIP

1. See some neat fossils.
2. Hang on to my lucky baseball hat.
3. Come home alive.

The guidebook had a map of the river showing what we might see at each mile. I flipped through the book, looking for rattlesnakes. I found the names of 14 other snakes I hadn't even heard of. I was figuring out which ones sounded poisonous, when Mom shouted, "Put the book down, and listen to how to live through the rapids." Remembering Goal Number Three, I put away the book and listened.

"The river can be dangerous," began Owen, "especially the rapids. And we'll meet some of the biggest in the world. Just wait until you see Lava Falls!" His eyes lit up. "It's a whopper!"

"Never take off your life jacket in the raft . . . even when we're not in the rapids," warned P.J.

They showed us how to squeeze onto the floor of the raft like fancy sardines and hold on to the side ropes. I looked at the names in black letters on our day-glow orange life jackets. They sounded silly . . . Red Hawk, Honeybunch, Nankoweap, Foo Foo, and Havasu to name a few. I was Foo Foo . . . and not too happy about it. But these names could instantly show who needed help or who was missing.

I looked around and suddenly felt very small. The cliffs, which had been quite low when we launched the raft, were slowly inching up. Rising layers of sand-colored rock grew on both sides of the river. The river itself was green and cold. It was so cold it chilled the bags of drinks the raft dragged along behind it. We also dragged bags for garbage. Sixteen thousand people lived on the river, camping on the sandy beaches each year. And they all carried out the garbage they made. We wouldn't even build campfires at night because as P.J. said, "The canyon is so special. We don't want to scar it."

Did I mention that it was hot? Well, it was . . . at least 100 degrees. As I splashed myself with icy river water, I suddenly saw two huge sheep staring at me from the shore. They were very still. Big horns curled out of their heads and looked as if they were listening with giant ears. And then, suddenly, they ran away . . . straight up a ragged cliff.

Just then I heard Owen holler, "Get ready for Badger Creek Rapid!"

We sat down, criss-crossing the raft and holding on to the ropes, just as we'd been taught.

Suddenly, the river foamed as we turned around and slid through the rapid backward! The rushing water swirled, lurched, and rose around us, playing with the big raft as if it were a tiny mouse. Mom looked scared. Dad looked even more scared. I laughed out loud. This was fun! I couldn't wait to see Lava Falls Rapid now. This trip might work out to be all right after all! Then I touched my head. It was bare. My lucky hat was gone . . . lost to the rapid forever! Goal Number Two was doomed.

That night I moped around the camp. I paid no attention to the mule deer that appeared on the North Rim of the canyon during dinner. I hardly looked at the bats fluttering around at dusk. I barely noticed the wicked-looking blood-red rocks that seemed to sneak closer when we weren't looking. I just thought about my lucky baseball hat.

"It may turn up, Foo Foo," said Dad.

All night I worried about going down the river without my hat. In the morning I was surprised to wake up in the canyon.

That was easy, considering what happened later that day. We'd drifted down the river with the motor off. It was so silent, so peaceful. Then suddenly, Owen steered over to a small beach.

"Everybody out of the raft," he ordered. "Go see the cavern on the far side of this beach," he said calmly. "Look in the rocks. You'll find some special things."

He was right. The rocks were carved with deep fossils that looked like sea squids. It was hard to believe, but once there was an ocean here. Then later, the river took billions of years to carve its slow, steady way through the rock to form this amazing canyon.

When we returned to the raft, I smugly checked off Goal Number One. Owen was smiling a sly smile.

"What's up?" I asked him.

He couldn't wait to tell me.

"When we were drifting along back there, I suddenly saw a rattlesnake's head pop up right next to Foo-Foo," he laughed.

I gasped so hard, I hiccupped.

"So I shooed you all out of the raft and over to the cavern. Then I flipped the snake over with the emergency oar . . . right onto the beach. He's there . . . under that brittlebush."

He pointed to a rattler with inky black diamonds printed along a fat, muscular body. Its pale eyes looked up at me like a ghostly mask. But the snake seemed tired and sad, coiled up in the shade. It looked beautiful, too. I wished it would rattle. I even wished I could touch it. From then on, I kept my eyes open for other rattlers. I wondered if they were all so beautiful. I never did find another one, but I saw other things.

Sometimes hikers lined high canyon ledges, like fire ants heading home.

Once a shimmering emerald-green hummingbird hovered over the raft, eating bits of sweet plum from my hand.

Another time, P.J. let me use our net to pluck things from the river. We found something almost every day. One day we fished up three juice cans, a water bottle, and a pair of baggy pants. We added them to our garbage bags to take out of the canyon.

One morning we drifted to a super-ugly black rock sticking right up in the middle of the river.

"Before each trip through Lava Falls, the youngest on board must kiss Vulcan's Anvil for good luck," announced Owen.

Everyone looked at me. I looked at Vulcan's Anvil and knew I didn't want to kiss it. But before I could complain, Owen had picked me up over the side of the raft. So I gave that gross rock a quick kiss and everyone cheered. Well after all, I didn't want to jinx our run through Lava! I wiped my mouth on my shirt about three times.

Suddenly, we knew we were nearing something enormous. We could hear it. We could feel it. Finally, we saw it. Lava Falls lay just ahead. Owen and P.J. stopped to plan their attack on the great rush of water. They studied the rapid, talking quietly. Finally, they both pointed thumbs up, and we all got back into the raft. Then we started toward the rapid.

I was sure everyone could hear my heart beat as the water swirled around us. We rode the rapid backward, as we did others. But this one was different. The engine rumbled, working hard to fight the great rush. Water crashed like thunder. Deep whirls sucked old trees and branches under. Water foamed and turned brown as it scraped dirt and rocks up from the bottom. The river flowed into the raft, drenching us all. We screamed with each bump on this roller coaster of water.

Just when it seemed the raft would flip over, and we'd all be sucked under the rocks and trees, Lava Falls Rapid was behind us. Everyone whooped and cheered.

Then suddenly, I saw it . . . a patch of blue in the water.

"Get the net," I yelled, but P.J. already had it. In a flash, he scooped up my lost lucky hat and flipped it onto my head. The hat had floated down the river with us! Cold water trickled out of the hat and onto my face.

"Miracles like this happen all the time in the canyon," said Owen patting my shoulder.

My mom was right all along. I was one of the lucky ones. Now I didn't want to leave the canyon. Who cared about New Jersey!

But the next afternoon, our time was up. As we walked out of the Grand Canyon at Diamond Creek, I checked off Goals Two and Three. Then I printed one more goal in giant letters.

MY GOALS FOR THIS TRIP
✓ 1. See some neat fossils.
✓ 2. Hang on to my lucky baseball hat.
3. Come home alive.
4. Come back and visit the Grand Canyon again.

The Story of Daedalus and Icarus

A retelling of a Greek myth

CHARACTERS

THREE CHORUS MEMBERS
DAEDALUS
ICARUS, the young son of Daedalus
KING MINOS
TWO GUARDS
THE MINOTAUR

ACT 1

Time:
Over two thousand years ago.

Setting:
A seashore on the island of Crete. In the background is a rock cliff. In the middle of the cliff is the entrance to a large maze. On each side of the entrance stands a GUARD, *holding a shield and spear.* DAEDALUS *and* KING MINOS *stand downstage, talking.* ICARUS *roams around the stage. From time to time, he stops to pick up and study a seashell. The* CHORUS MEMBERS *are lined up in front of the rock at stage left. Before speaking, each* CHORUS MEMBER *takes a step forward. After speaking, he or she steps back in line.*

CHORUS MEMBER 1:
(Pointing to DAEDALUS*)*

Daedalus is a famous artist, inventor, and builder. He is known throughout the land for the clever things he creates. His statues are so lifelike they seem to breathe. His palaces are so magnificent, they rival those of the gods on Mount Olympus. His fame has reached even to the island of Crete.

CHORUS MEMBER 2:
(Pointing to KING MINOS*)*

King Minos, who rules Crete, is a tyrant—a cruel and wicked man. He offered Daedalus a great deal of money to build a prison for a horrible beast called the *Minotaur*. The Minotaur has the body of a man and the head of a bull. For years, he has terrified the people of Crete. But the Minotaur is also the son of King Minos' wife, and so the king does not want to kill him. Daedalus accepted King Minos' offer.

(Pointing to the walled maze)

To hold the Minotaur, he has built this splendid maze, called the *Labyrinth*. The soldiers are getting ready to bring the Minotaur to the Labyrinth.

DAEDALUS:
(To KING MINOS*)*

My Labyrinth has hundreds of twisted and tangled paths. Anyone who enters it soon becomes hopelessly lost. Once inside, the Minotaur can never escape. Indeed, only *I* know how to find the way out.

KING MINOS:
(With impatience)

Yes, yes. So you have said before.

DAEDALUS:

If you doubt me, ask your soldiers who have tried to solve the puzzle. If I had not saved them, they would all still be inside the Labyrinth.

CHORUS MEMBER 3:
(Pointing to ICARUS*)*

When Daedalus came to Crete, he brought along his son, Icarus. Icarus is brave and smart, but he often acts and speaks without thinking.

ICARUS *reaches the entrance to the maze. He glances at his father, then starts to go inside.*

DAEDALUS:

Icarus! No! How many times have I told you that you must never go inside the Labyrinth! Remember the soldiers?

ICARUS:
(Laughing)

Oh, Father! I am much smarter than a common soldier. I'm sure that *I* can find my way through your maze.

DAEDALUS:

If you were truly smart, you would learn to listen to those who are older and wiser.

ICARUS *skips to his father's side. An angry roar fills the air. The* GUARDS *tremble, their spears rattling against their shields. The* CHORUS MEMBERS *scramble behind the rock.*

DAEDALUS:
(Pulling ICARUS *near)*

The Minotaur!

KING MINOS:

Of course. You say that the beast can never escape from this Labyrinth, but as yet I have seen no proof of your claim.

(Turning toward the GUARDS*)*

Bring the Minotaur here!

The GUARDS *exit, still trembling. From offstage, the roars become louder and angrier. They are mixed with the shouts and cries of the* GUARDS.

FIRST GUARD:

Move him this way! Quickly! No, don't let him turn!

SECOND GUARD:

Yes! Yes! I know. Watch him! Watch him!

The MINOTAUR *enters, roaring and stomping. His hands are tied behind his back.* KING MINOS *and* DAEDALUS *take a few steps backward.* ICARUS *remains where he is, watching the action with excitement.*

DAEDALUS:
(Grabbing his son's robe and tugging him backward)
Icarus!

ICARUS:

I want to help!

The GUARDS dance around the MINOTAUR, lunging at him with their spears. They force him inside the Labyrinth, and he turns and disappears down a pathway. As the MINOTAUR's roars become more and more faint, everyone on stage breathes deeply. The CHORUS MEMBERS come out from behind the rock and line up once more. The GUARDS take their positions. ICARUS runs to the entrance and peeks inside.

CHORUS MEMBER 1:

And so the Minotaur was trapped in the Labyrinth. With this, Daedalus thought his work was finished.

CHORUS MEMBER 2:

But remember, King Minos is a wicked man. He cannot be trusted.

DAEDALUS:

Come, Icarus, it is time for us to say good-bye to King Minos. We must prepare to sail for home.

KING MINOS:
(Smiling slyly)

I regret that your plans will have to change. As you have told me, you are the only person who knows how to escape from the Labyrinth. Do you really think that I can let you leave this island with such valuable knowledge? What if my enemies find out the secret? What if they release the Minotaur? Oh, no. I cannot risk that.

(Motioning to the GUARDS)

Come, take these two to the tower and lock them up!

The GUARDS *start toward* DAEDALUS *and* ICARUS. ICARUS *charges them, swinging his fists. The first* GUARD *smiles and takes* ICARUS *firmly by the arm. The second* GUARD *points a spear at* DAEDALUS.

DAEDALUS:

Icarus! Do as they say.

ICARUS:

But Father . . . !

The GUARDS *march their prisoners offstage.*

CHORUS MEMBER 3:

Poor Daedalus! Poor Icarus! What will happen to them now?

The lights dim.

ACT 2

Time:
A year later.

Setting:
Inside a gloomy high tower on the coast of Crete. DAEDALUS *sits on a wooden bench, head in hands.* ICARUS *stands beside a large window. Through the window, several seabirds can be seen soaring through the air. The* CHORUS MEMBERS *stand in shadows downstage.*

CHORUS MEMBER 1:

King Minos had made Daedalus and Icarus prisoners in this high tower near the sea. The have only a pile of straw to sleep on. Their only visitors are the Guards who bring them food.

CHORUS MEMBER 2:

(Pointing to DAEDALUS*)*

CHORUS MEMBER 3:
(Pointing to ICARUS*)*

ICARUS:
(Turning to DAEDALUS*)*

DAEDALUS:
(Looking at his son with a sad smile)

ICARUS:
(Sighing)

(He turns back to watch the birds.)

At first, Daedalus did not worry. After all, he was known far and wide for his cleverness. He was sure that he could find a way to escape the tower. Alas, all of his clever plans for escape have failed, and failure has made him very unhappy.

He has given up hope.

But Icarus has not given up hope for escape. Each day he stands at the window and watches for ships.

Come, look, father! There is a ship far away on the horizon. Perhaps we can signal it.

With what, my son? We cannot make a fire. We have no cloth to wave. And you know that King Minos has promised death to anyone who helps us to escape. What ship's captain or crew will defy the king?

You are right, Father. We can never leave this place.

But at least come watch the beautiful birds. They move so easily through the sky.

DAEDALUS:
(Walking to the window)

Yes, they are beautiful.

(He watches for a moment, then claps his hands and laugh.)

Of course! I've been blind! Thank you, my son, for opening my eyes. King Minos may block us from leaving by sea, but he does not control the sky.

(Slapping ICARUS on the back)

We will fly out of this prison!

ICARUS:

Oh, Father, how can we fly? We are not birds.

DAEDALUS:

We are not birds, but we *can* fly! You will see!

The stage goes dark. A spotlight focuses on the CHORUS MEMBERS.

CHORUS MEMBER 1:

Daedalus began to place bits of bread from their meals on the windowsill. Soon the birds were flocking to the window and fighting among themselves for the bread. As they squabbled, feathers flew everywhere, and Icarus hurried to collect as many as possible.

CHORUS MEMBER 2:

Daedalus showed Icarus how to arrange the feathers in order of size. Using a needle he made from a piece of bone and thread taken from his robe, he sewed together the feathers, shaping them into wings. He used leather from his belt and sandals to make straps and harnesses, and he attached the wings to the harnesses with candle wax.

CHORUS MEMBER 3:

Then one day at sunrise, Daedalus woke
Icarus.

The stage lightens. Icarus is asleep on the pile of straw. DAEDALUS *is standing
nearby. He is wearing one pair of wings and holding a smaller pair.*

DAEDALUS:

Come, my son, your wings are ready. Let
me help you put them on.

ICARUS *gets up, rubbing the sleep from his eyes. He stands as* DAEDALUS *slips the
wings over his arms.*

ICARUS:

I'm afraid, Father. I don't know how to
make the wings work.

DAEDALUS:

First, spread them like this.

(Spreading his arms and wings wide)

Then slowly move them up and down.

ICARUS:

(Flapping his wings and moving around the stage, slowly at first, then faster and faster)

Look at me! I'm flying! I'm flying. Let's leave now!

(He starts for the tower window.)

DAEDALUS:

No, not yet. Before we leave, you must listen closely to what I tell you.

ICARUS:

(Dropping his wings to his sides)

Yes, Father, I will listen.

DAEDALUS:

Good, because your life depends on doing as I say. You must stay close to me. If you fly too low, the sea water will make your feathers heavy, and you will sink into the water. If you fly too high, the sun will melt the candle wax and your wings will fall off. Do you understand?

ICARUS:

I understand, Father.

DAEDALUS:

Then let us fly before the guards come with our food.

They flap their wings and circle around the stage several times, then each goes to the window and leaps out.

DAEDALUS:

(Offstage)

Remember, stay close to me and do what I said.

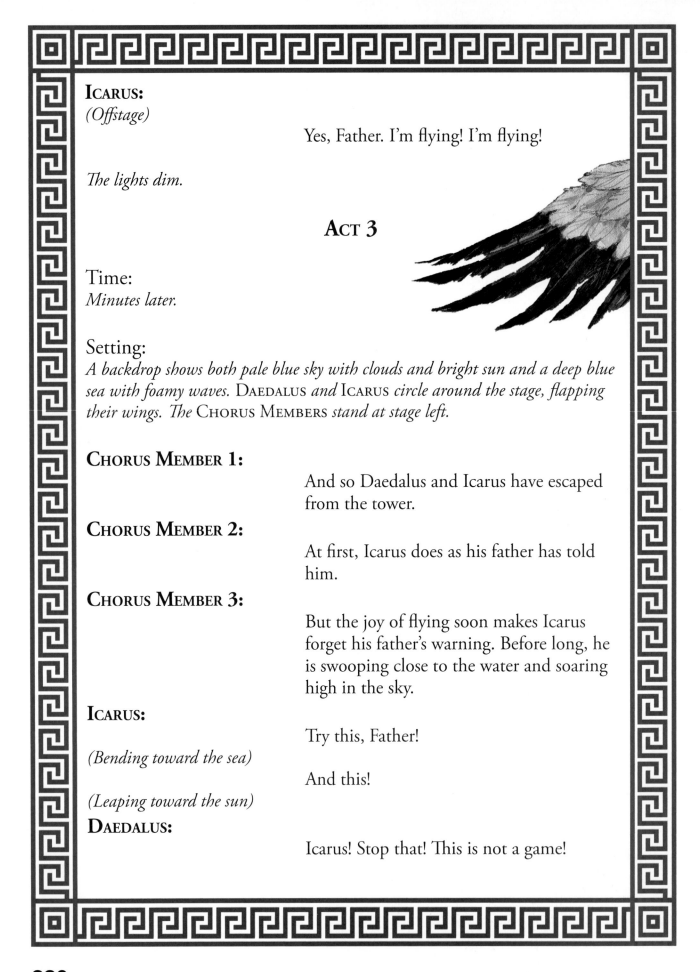

ICARUS:
(Offstage)

Yes, Father. I'm flying! I'm flying!

The lights dim.

ACT 3

Time:
Minutes later.

Setting:
A backdrop shows both pale blue sky with clouds and bright sun and a deep blue sea with foamy waves. DAEDALUS *and* ICARUS *circle around the stage, flapping their wings. The* CHORUS MEMBERS *stand at stage left.*

CHORUS MEMBER 1:

And so Daedalus and Icarus have escaped from the tower.

CHORUS MEMBER 2:

At first, Icarus does as his father has told him.

CHORUS MEMBER 3:

But the joy of flying soon makes Icarus forget his father's warning. Before long, he is swooping close to the water and soaring high in the sky.

ICARUS:

(Bending toward the sea)

(Leaping toward the sun)

Try this, Father!

And this!

DAEDALUS:

Icarus! Stop that! This is not a game!

220

(ICARUS *gets closer and closer to the sun.*)

What are you doing? Come back!

ICARUS:

(Stopping suddenly. For a moment, he stands with his wings outstretched. Then the wings begin to slip from his arms)

Father! The wax is melting! I'm falling!

ICARUS *sinks slowly to the floor.* DAEDALUS, *flapping his wings, circles him.*

DAEDALUS:

My son! My son!

The lights dim, then the stage goes dark. A spotlight shows the CHORUS MEMBERS.

CHORUS MEMBER 1:

Icarus disappeared into the dark sea.

CHORUS MEMBER 2:

Daedalus searched and searched for his son, but all he found were feathers floating on the water. Weeping bitter tears, he flew on until he reached land.

CHORUS MEMBER 3:

There he built a temple to Apollo, the Greek god of youth and life. And on the walls of the temple, Daedalus placed his wings, never to fly again.

Curtain closes.

The End